The Mayo Clinic Kids' Cookbook

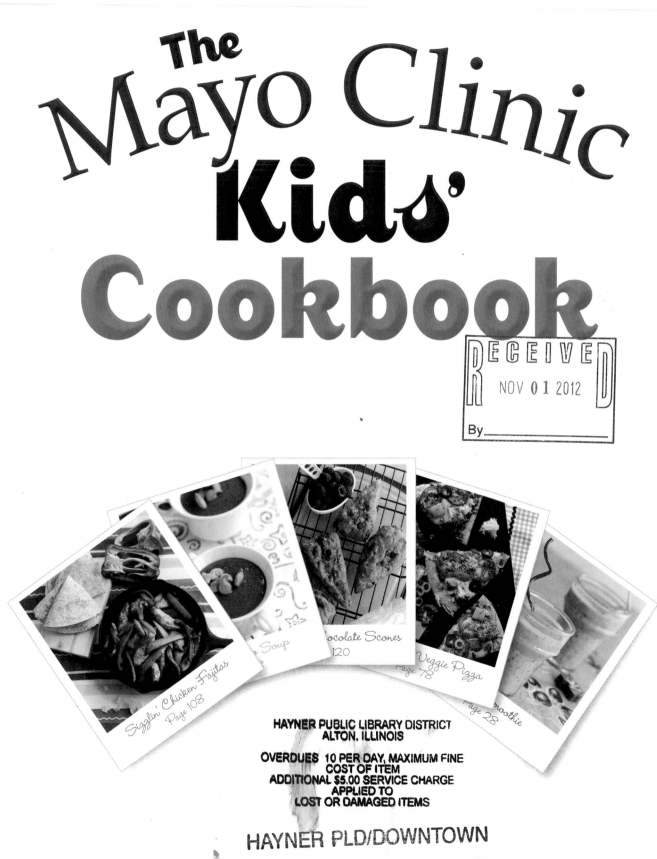

Sizzlin' Chicken Fajitas
Page 108

Soup

ocolate Scones
120

Veggie Pizza
Page 78

moothie
28

The Mayo Clinic Kids' Cookbook

50 Favorite Recipes for Fun and Healthy Eating

Good Books

Intercourse, PA 17534 • 800-762-7171 • www.GoodBooks.com

MAYO CLINIC

Medical Editor
Donald Hensrud, M.D.

Associate Medical Editor
Jennifer Nelson, R.D.

Managing Editor
Leigh McKinney

Senior Product Manager, Books
Christopher Frye

Director, Health Information
Jay Maxwell

Proofreaders
Miranda Attlesey, Donna Hanson, Julie Maas

Although the analysts and the editors have attempted full accuracy in the nutritional data and analyses included in this cookbook, many variables (including the variations related to particular brands, to the refinement of products, and to the exact amounts of ingredients) could result in the analyses being approximate.

Because many factors influence your health, please check with your health care expert before making substantial changes in what you eat.

MAYO, MAYO CLINIC and the Mayo triple-shield logo are marks of Mayo Foundation for Medical Education and Research.

© 2012 Mayo Foundation for Medical Education and Research

GOOD BOOKS

Publisher
Merle Good

Executive Editor
Phyllis Pellman Good

Assistant Publisher
Kate Good

Published by Good Books

Photographs and recipes © by Good Books, Intercourse, PA 17534
All photography by Jeremy Hess Photographers/JH
Design by Cliff Snyder

ISBN: 978-1-56148-751-6
Library of Congress Control Number: 2012933706

Publisher's Cataloging-in-Publication data
The Mayo Clinic kids' cookbook : 50 favorite recipes for fun and healthy eating / [Mayo Clinic].
   p.cm.
   Includes index.
   ISBN 978-1-56148-751-6
1. Cooking --Juvenile literature. 2. Nutrition --Juvenile literature. 3. Food --Juvenile literature. I. Mayo Clinic. II. The Mayo Clinic kids' cookbook : fifty favorite recipes for fun and healthy eating. III. Title.
TX652.5 M39 2012
[641] --dc23   2012933706

First Edition

The recipes in this book are adapted from recipes in *Fix-It and Enjoy-It Healthy Cookbook: 400 Great Stove-Top and Oven Recipes*, by Phyllis Pellman Good, with nutritional expertise from Mayo Clinic.

Good Books wishes to thank Phyllis Pellman Good for her supervision of this project; Rebecca Good Fennimore and Kate Good, who oversaw the photography of the recipes included in the book; Bonne di Tomo and Lisa, the food-stylists for the project; Jeremy Hess for his photography; and Margaret High for editing the recipes, selected by Rebecca Good Fennimore.

If you would like more copies of this book, contact Good Books, Intercourse, PA 17534; 800/762-7171; www.GoodBooks.com

For bulk sales to employers, member groups and health-related companies, contact Mayo Clinic Health Solutions, 200 First St. SW, Rochester, MN 55905, or SpecialSalesMayoBooks@mayo.edu

Table of Contents

Italian Flags (Caprese Salad)
Page 36

Tuna Flippers
Page 102

Wild West Pasta
Page 86

Wacky Chocolate Cake
Page 122

Frozen Dream Pops
Page 30

Welcome to the Kitchen— and to Cooking!

Hey Kids—

Now you can make meals you like! Use this book to put great food on your plate — and on the plates of everyone else at the table — for breakfast, lunch and dinner. And for an after-school snack, too.

The food you eat every day is called your "diet." The word *diet* actually means "way of living." A healthy diet can be pictured in many ways, but it's often found in the shape of a pyramid. That's what Mayo Clinic uses to show how the pieces of a healthy diet fit together. The base of the pyramid is made up of foods that should make up the biggest piece of your diet. The foods you should eat in smaller amounts are shown in the smaller parts of the pyramid.

And don't forget exercise! It's an important part of staying healthy, and that's why it's right in the middle of the pyramid.

Of course, no one food can provide all the nutrients you need, so it's important to eat a variety of foods from all of the food groups.

The pyramid and the plate on page 7 give you the same information, just in two different ways.

Before you choose a recipe to make, think of your empty dinner plate. How are you going to fill it?

Sweets

Fats

Protein and Dairy

Grains

Daily Physical Activity

Fruits

Vegetables

Mayo Clinic Healthy Weight Pyramid

First imagine a line through the center of the plate that divides it in half.

You're going to fill one of those halves with fruits and vegetables. The more bright colors on this half of your plate, the better.

Look for recipes for this part of your plate in Chapter 1, "Fruit-tastic," and in Chapter 2, "Veggies Rule."

Now imagine a line running across the unfilled part of the plate. Fill in the top section with food made from recipes in Chapter 4, "Plenty of Protein." And the bottom section is for food made from recipes in Chapter 3, "Great Grains."

Enjoy some "Tiny Treats" from Chapter 5 after you've finished the food on your dinner plate. Or when you come home from school or after a game.

One more step before you cook. Write a grocery list of all the food you'll need to make the recipes you've chosen. Then ask your parents if you may go along to the grocery store to help shop for the ingredients. You can help to choose what you'll need to make the meal.

Eat a little snack before you go so you aren't hungry while you shop. Stick a banana in your pocket, or put a bunch of grapes in a little bag, to eat on the way.

Now it's time to cook! Welcome to the kitchen and to *The Mayo Clinic Kids' Cookbook*!

Ask your mom or dad to keep a bowl of fresh fruit on your kitchen counter or in the fridge all the time. You can help yourself whenever you're hungry!

For Adult Helpers

Take your children a step beyond hot dogs and mac and cheese. Let them begin to cook using recipes and ingredients that contribute to their health — and to your whole family's well-being.

Help your children understand the ideal way to fill a dinner plate — and to plan a meal — by following the dinner-plate drawing on page 7. Also teach your children how to keep food safe by cooking it thoroughly and refrigerating it promptly. Be sure to emphasize frequent hand-washing too.

A few other suggestions:

1 Cooking is a natural activity for kids. Allow your own sense of wonder to be renewed — along with the child's!

2 Be willing to yield your space to the child who is cooking. While a child should never be left alone to cook, be prepared to let the child occupy your kitchen as fully as necessary.

3 Try as much as possible to serve as a coach, rather than being in charge.

4 You'll need patience. Efficiency is not the highest value in this experience.

5 You'll need flexibility. Kids like to experiment with new ingredients and different methods than those that are given. Through it all, remember to be an encourager!

6 Realize that children enjoy the tactile experience of cooking. Touching and tasting along the way is normal. But steer your child away from touching and tasting uncooked foods containing raw eggs (like cookie dough and cake batters) and uncooked meats.

7 Most importantly — let family and friends know that your child prepared the food that they're eating!

Playing the Game!

Next to each recipe in this cookbook, you'll see a drawing of a dinner plate with different colored sections (and a glass of milk).

Inside each section is a bunch of circles.

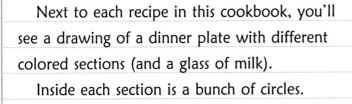

Some of the circles are colored. Those colored circles mean that you're getting foods from that food group when you eat that recipe.

The goal of the game is to choose recipes that help you eat the kinds of foods you need each day, in the right amounts, so that your body has what it needs to be strong and healthy.

Here are the total number of circles a child should aim for in a day (the USDA food groups for kids ages 7 to 12 were used to determine the ideal number of circles):

Fruits – 4+ circles

Vegetables – 4+ circles

Grains – 6 circles

Protein and Dairy – 5 circles total

Fats – 5 circles

Sweets – You don't need sweets, but you'll see a circle if the recipe includes sweets.

Cooking Abbreviations

t. or tsp. = teaspoon
T. or Tbsp. = tablespoon
c. = cup
pt. = pint
qt. = quart
oz. = ounce
lb. = pound
pkg. = package

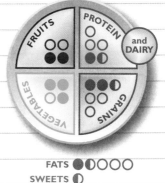

So, for example, you might make a recipe from the vegetable chapter, so that recipe will show colored circles in the vegetables part of your plate.

But it probably has colored circles in other sections of your plate, too. For example, if you make "Fiesta Chicken Salad," on page 40, you'll have colored circles in the vegetables part of your plate, plus in the grains (because of the pita bread) and protein (because of the chicken) sections.

Add up all the colored circles for all of the dishes you make for a meal, and see how many circles (or servings) you will have eaten in each section of your plate by the time you finish!

Fiesta Chicken Salad
Page 40

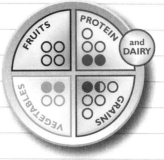

Fiesta Chicken Salad
Nutritional Information

This way you can see how many circles — and which kinds of foods — you might plan to eat at another meal or snack. Your goal is to choose meals and snacks that fill up the circles you should eat on most days.

Conversion Chart

A pinch/dash = less than ⅛ teaspoon
1 tablespoon = 3 teaspoons
⅛ cup = 2 tablespoons
¼ cup = 4 tablespoons
⅓ cup = 5 tablespoons + 1 teaspoon
½ cup = 8 tablespoons
⅔ cup = 10 tablespoons + 2 teaspoons
¾ cup = 12 tablespoons
8 fluid ounces = 1 cup
1 pint = 2 cups
1 quart = 2 pints
1 quart = 4 cups
1 gallon = 4 quarts
16 ounces = 1 pound

How Much Is a Serving?

When you really, really like something, it can be hard to stop eating it, right? Well, you don't need to worry about eating too many fruits and vegetables. Your body likes and needs them.

In fact, here's an idea — when you begin your meal, start by eating the vegetables and fruits on your plate. When you've taken a good bite out of them, then start eating the foods in the grains and protein sections of your plate.

Here are a few pictures to give you an idea of how big one serving (or one circle on your plate) is:

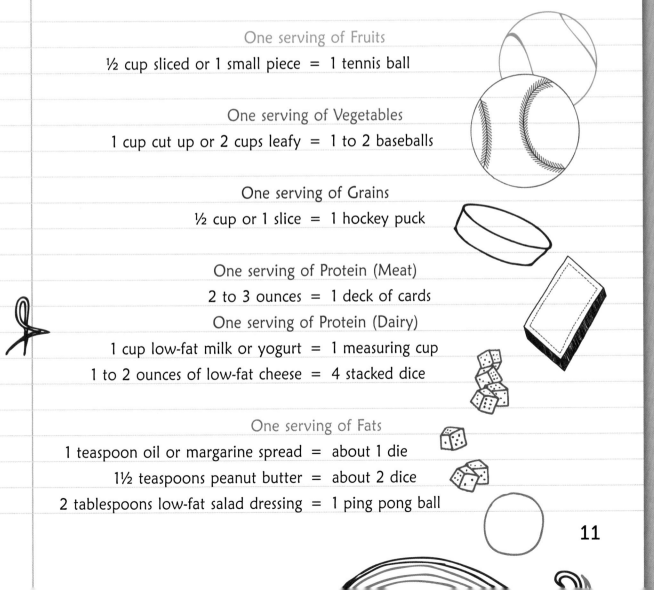

One serving of Fruits

½ cup sliced or 1 small piece = 1 tennis ball

One serving of Vegetables

1 cup cut up or 2 cups leafy = 1 to 2 baseballs

One serving of Grains

½ cup or 1 slice = 1 hockey puck

One serving of Protein (Meat)

2 to 3 ounces = 1 deck of cards

One serving of Protein (Dairy)

1 cup low-fat milk or yogurt = 1 measuring cup

1 to 2 ounces of low-fat cheese = 4 stacked dice

One serving of Fats

1 teaspoon oil or margarine spread = about 1 die

1½ teaspoons peanut butter = about 2 dice

2 tablespoons low-fat salad dressing = 1 ping pong ball

Equipment List

Aluminum foil – A paper-thin sheet of metal used to cover food items.

Colander – A bowl with holes in it used to drain water or other liquids from foods.

Cookie (baking) sheet – A flat metal sheet used for baking cookies.

Cooking spray – A liquid you spray on the inside of a baking dish or sheet so food won't stick.

Cutting board – A board that you chop or cut ingredients on.

Food thermometer – A tool to check the temperature of a food to see if it's cooked enough.

Glass measuring cup – A glass cup, used to measure liquids, with measurements printed on its side.

Jar with a tightfitting lid – Used to shake ingredients together until well mixed, such as salad dressings.

Kitchen shears – A type of scissors used to cut herbs and other food items.

Ladle – A long-handled dipper used for transferring liquid from one container to another.

Measuring cups – Cups in different sizes, used to measure dry ingredients.

Measuring spoons – Spoons in different sizes used to measure small amounts of liquid or dry ingredients.

Microwave-safe glass bowl – Cookware made of glass that is safe to use in the microwave. Metal items are not safe to use in a microwave.

Mixing bowls – Bowls of different sizes in which you mix ingredients together.

Plastic wrap – A sheet of plastic that covers food.

Potholders – Mittens or pads to hold hot pots, pans, lids and baking sheets.

Rolling pin – A roller used to flatten an item such as dough for a pie crust.

Rubber spatula – A narrow, flexible blade used for cleaning food out of containers.

Safety can opener – A tool to open cans that creates a safe, smooth edge around the opening.

Sealable plastic bag – A plastic bag that can be sealed tightly.

Shallow bowl – A bowl with short sides for dipping foods into.

Timer – A tool that keeps time as you cook.

Safety Tips

1. Make sure an adult is always nearby when you're cooking. Ask for help when you have questions or if a container is too heavy or too hot to handle.
2. Wash your hands with warm, soapy water before you start cooking. Wash your hands right after working with raw meat or eggs.
3. Wash fresh fruits and vegetables under running water.
4. Use separate cutting boards for raw meat and fresh fruits and vegetables.
5. Wear clothing without baggy sleeves. Tie back your hair if it's long.
6. Use potholders to handle hot items.
7. Clean up any spills right away.
8. Have an adult help you when a recipe tells you to use a knife.
9. Use microwave-safe containers. Metal cannot be safely used in a microwave.
10. Put ingredients back into the fridge, cupboards or drawers when you're done using them.
11. When you are finished cooking, gather together all of the dirty dishes and utensils. Wipe the counter and work area. Wash the dirty dishes and help clean up the mess. (That will encourage your mom or dad to let you cook again! Plus it's part of cooking.)
12. Use a food thermometer to check the temperature of cooked meat, poultry and egg dishes.

Toothpick – A slim piece of wood or plastic used to test if a cake is done, to serve bite-sized food, or to remove food from between your teeth.

Trivet – A block of wood, metal or tile on which you set a hot pot or dish to protect the table or countertop.

Twist tie – A short, paper-covered wire used to twist around a bag to close it.

Whisk – A utensil made of wire loops, used for mixing liquid ingredients together.

Wooden spoon – A tool used for mixing and stirring almost any kind of food.

13

Jack-o'-Lantern Soup
Page 20

*Polka-Dot
Banana Muffins*
Page 22

Fruity Smoothie
Page 28

Berry Breakfast Parfait
Page 16

Frozen Dream Pops
Page 30

Chapter 1
Fruit-tastic

Berry Breakfast Parfait

SWEETS ◗

Makes 4 servings • Prep Time: 15 minutes

INGREDIENTS

2 cups fat-free, low-calorie vanilla yogurt

¼ teaspoon ground cinnamon, *if your granola doesn't have cinnamon in it*

1 cup sliced strawberries

½ cup blueberries

½ cup raspberries

1 cup low-fat granola

EQUIPMENT

Small bowl

Knife

Cutting board

Medium bowl

Wooden spoon

4 tall sundae glasses

1. Put yogurt in the small bowl. If you want to add cinnamon, mix it in now.

2. Ask an adult to help you slice the strawberries. Put in the medium bowl.

3. Add blueberries and raspberries to the medium bowl. Gently mix fruit together.

4. To make a parfait, put ¼ cup fruit mixture in the bottom of a sundae glass.

5. Add 2 tablespoons granola.

6. Top with ¼ cup yogurt.

7. Repeat layering the fruit, granola and yogurt one more time.

8. Repeat with the other 3 glasses.

9. Top each parfait with berries and a sprinkling of granola. Serve right away.

This also makes a great dessert!

Fruit Slushy

Makes 8 servings   •   Prep Time: 10 minutes
Freezing Time: 8 hours or overnight   •   Thawing Time: 1-2 hours

INGREDIENTS

6-ounce can frozen orange
   juice concentrate

1 cup hot water from the tap

4 bananas, sliced

2 tablespoons lemon juice

15-ounce can crushed
   unsweetened pineapple
   with juice

EQUIPMENT

Mixing bowl with lid or
   plastic wrap

Wooden spoon

Knife

Cutting board

Safety can opener

8 glasses

1. In a large bowl, combine frozen concentrate and hot water. Using the wooden spoon, stir and mash concentrate until it's dissolved in the water.

2. Ask an adult to help you slice the bananas. Add the slices to the mixing bowl.

3. Add lemon juice and crushed pineapple (with its juice) to the mixing bowl, too. Mix gently.

4. Cover the bowl and freeze for 8 hours or overnight.

5. One or 2 hours before you want to serve, take the bowl out of the freezer. Let the mixture thaw until it's slushy.

6. Spoon into glasses and serve.

Remember this as a snack on a hot summer afternoon!

Jack-o'-Lantern Soup

Makes 6 servings • Prep Time: 30 minutes • Cooking Time: 30 minutes

FATS ●○○○○

INGREDIENTS

1 cup chopped onion

2 tablespoons olive oil

1 teaspoon curry powder

4 cups fat-free, low-sodium chicken or vegetable broth

15-ounce can solid-pack pumpkin

½ cup unsweetened applesauce

2 tablespoons plain fat-free yogurt

EQUIPMENT

Cutting board

Knife

Large saucepan with lid

Wooden spoon

Safety can opener

Stick blender

6 soup bowls

1. With an adult helping you, chop onion. Set it aside.

2. Ask an adult to help you heat oil in the saucepan. Add onion and curry powder. Stir and cook until the onion is getting soft, at least 5 minutes.

3. Carefully pour broth into the saucepan. Keep the heat on medium and don't cover the pot. You want the broth to come to a boil, which could take 15-25 minutes.

4. When the broth is boiling (bubbling strongly), turn off the heat. Open the can of pumpkin. Carefully spoon the pumpkin into the hot broth. Add the applesauce.

5. With an adult's help, puree the soup with the stick blender.

6. Spoon soup into bowls and top each with 1 teaspoon plain yogurt.

When you "puree" the soup, you make it smooth and velvety.

Sometimes "stick blenders" are called "immersion blenders." Check with your parents to see if you have one. If not, you can use a regular "stand blender." You'll need an adult to help you, whichever kind you have.

Did you know that pumpkin is actually a fruit, not a vegetable? But because pumpkin provides carbohydrates, it's counted in the grains group.

Polka-Dot Banana Muffins

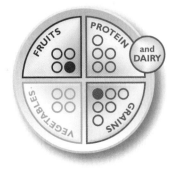

Makes 12 servings • Prep Time: 10 minutes
Standing Time: 10 minutes • Cooking Time: 20 minutes

INGREDIENTS

1 cup of your favorite dry bran cereal

¼ cup skim milk

1 cup all-purpose white flour

1 teaspoon baking soda

¼ teaspoon salt

2 very ripe bananas, peeled

6 tablespoons egg substitute

¼ cup agave nectar *or* honey

¼ cup unsweetened applesauce

¾ cup raisins or craisins (dried cranberries)

EQUIPMENT

12-cup muffin pan

Cooking spray

Large mixing bowl

Wooden spoon

Potato masher

Medium mixing bowl

Potholders

Cooling rack

1. Preheat oven to 375° F. Spray each cup in the muffin pan with cooking spray.

2. In a large mixing bowl, combine cereal with milk. Let stand 10 minutes to soften.

3. Now stir in flour, baking soda and salt.

4. In a separate bowl, mash bananas with potato masher. Add egg substitute, honey and applesauce. Mash and mix again.

5. Stir raisins into the banana mixture.

6. Add the banana mixture to the cereal mixture. Stir gently, just until the cereal-flour mixture is all wet. (If you mix too much, the muffins will be tough.)

7. Spoon the batter evenly into the 12 muffin cups.

8. Ask an adult to help you put the pan in the oven. Bake for 20 minutes, or until a toothpick stuck into the centers of several muffins comes out clean.

9. Use potholders to take the muffin pan out of the oven and place it on a cooling rack. Let the muffins cool for 3 minutes. Carefully remove muffins from the pan.

10. Serve warm or at room temperature.

Use your overripe bananas to make these muffins!.

Children younger than 1 year old shouldn't eat honey. Use agave nectar instead if a baby might be eating some of the muffins.

Mini Strawberry Shortcakes

Makes 8 servings • Prep Time: 20 minutes
Cooking Time: 12 minutes • Cooling Time: 7 minutes

FATS ●○○○○

INGREDIENTS

1 quart (4 cups) fresh strawberries *or* other berries

3 tablespoons honey *or* agave nectar, *divided*

1½ cups whole-wheat pastry flour

1 teaspoon baking powder

⅛ teaspoon salt

¼ cup trans-fat-free margarine

2 egg whites *or* ¼ cup egg substitute

½ cup skim milk

EQUIPMENT

12-cup muffin pan

Cooking spray

2 medium mixing bowls

Knife

Cutting board

Pastry cutter

Small bowl

Wooden spoon

Potholders

1. Preheat the oven to 425° F. Spray the muffin pan with cooking spray.

2. With an adult helping you, remove the leaves and stems from the strawberries. Ask the adult to help you slice the berries into one of the mixing bowls. Stir in 2 tablespoons honey. Set aside.

3. In the other mixing bowl, combine flour, baking powder, salt and 1 tablespoon honey.

4. Cut the margarine into the dry ingredients with a pastry cutter until the mixture turns into pieces that are about the size of peas.

5. In a small bowl, beat egg substitute and milk together.

6. Stir the wet ingredients into the flour mixture just until everything is wet. Too much stirring will make the shortcakes hard and dry.

7. Spoon the batter evenly into 8 muffin cups — they should be ⅔ full of batter. (If you have empty muffin cups, fill each about halfway with water, so the pan doesn't warp from the oven's heat.)

8. With an adult's help, put the muffin pan in the oven. Bake for 12 minutes, or until the shortcakes are golden.

9. Using potholders, and your adult helper, take the muffin pan out of the oven. Allow the cakes to cool in the pan for 7 minutes. Then remove them from the pan.

10. You can serve them warm, or put them on a rack to cool completely. When you're ready to serve the shortcakes, ask an adult to help you use a knife to split the shortcakes in half horizontally.

11. Lay 2 halves in a dessert bowl. Spoon the berries over the cake halves. Repeat this, using the other cakes and berries. Serve right away!

Babies shouldn't eat honey. Use agave nectar instead.

Fruit 'n' Puddin'

Makes 6 servings • Prep Time: 30 minutes

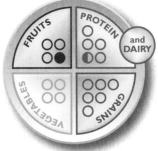

INGREDIENTS

20-ounce can unsweetened
   pineapple chunks

Water

1 small package sugar-free
   vanilla instant pudding
   mix

1 firm banana

1 tablespoon lemon juice

1½ cups grapes

1 pear *or* peach

1 cup blueberries, *or* ½ cup
   blueberries and ½ cup
   raspberries

EQUIPMENT

Colander

Liquid measuring cup

Safety can opener

Small mixing bowl

Whisk

Wooden spoon

Knife

Cutting board

Serving bowl with lid
   or plastic wrap

1. Set the strainer over the liquid measuring cup. Open the can of pineapple. Pour the pineapple into the colander so the juice drains into the measuring cup.

2. Add water to the pineapple juice to make a total of 1 cup of liquid.

3. In the mixing bowl, combine the liquid with the pudding mix. Whisk until thickened.

4. Ask an adult to help you slice the banana. Place the slices in the serving bowl.

5. Add the lemon juice to the banana slices and stir gently. With an adult helping you, cut each grape in half. Add them to the serving bowl.

6. With an adult helping you, cut up the pear or peach, but do not peel. Add to the serving bowl.

7. Add the berries to the serving bowl. Gently mix the fruit together.

8. Add the pudding to the fruit. Stir one more time, very gently.

9. Put the bowl in the refrigerator, covered, until you're ready to serve.

Fruity Smoothie

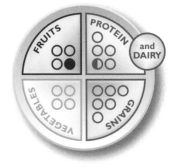

Makes 4 servings • Prep Time: 10 minutes

INGREDIENTS

1 cup frozen unsweetened strawberries

1 cup frozen unsweetened peaches

¾ cup frozen unsweetened blueberries

1 large ripe banana

1 cup fat-free, low-calorie peach *or* strawberry yogurt

1 cup skim milk

EQUIPMENT

Blender

Spatula

4 glasses

1. Put all the ingredients in the blender.

2. With an adult helping you, process in the blender until the mixture is smooth. Stop the blender and scrape the sides so everything gets well mixed.

3. Pour the smoothie into serving glasses.

Stop! Don't throw those overripe bananas away! Turn them into a smoothie.

Frozen Dream Pops

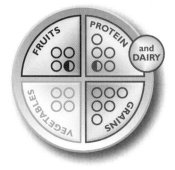

Makes 8 servings • Thawing Time: 10-20 minutes
Prep Time: 15 minutes • Freezing Time: 6 hours

INGREDIENTS

6-ounce can unsweetened
 orange juice concentrate

2 cups low-fat plain yogurt

1 teaspoon vanilla

EQUIPMENT

Mixing bowl

Wooden spoon

8 popsicle molds or
 3-ounce paper cups +
 foil + wooden sticks

1. Set the can of orange juice concentrate on the counter with the lid off to thaw for 10-20 minutes.

2. Pour or spoon it into the mixing bowl. Add the yogurt and the vanilla. Mix well.

3. Pour the mixture into 8 popsicle molds or paper cups, dividing it equally among them. If you're using cups, cover each with a square of foil. Then poke a stick through the foil into the yogurt mixture.

4. Freeze until solid, about 6 hours.

Bring these out when you have friends over!

Italian Oven Fries
Page 66

Cheesy Zucchini Caterpillar
Page 72

Italian Flags
(Caprese Salad)
Page 36

Tasty Tomato Soup
Page 48

Asian Green Beans
Page 58

Chapter 2

Veggies Rule

ABC Salad

Makes 6 servings • Prep Time: 30 minutes

INGREDIENTS

2 of your favorite kind of apples

3 cups fresh broccoli florets

⅓ cup craisins (dried cranberries)

¼ cup chopped walnuts, *if you like; not included in nutritional analysis*

1 tablespoon chopped red onion, *if you like; not included in nutritional analysis*

½ cup fat-free, low-calorie vanilla yogurt

EQUIPMENT

Cutting board

Knife

Medium salad bowl

Wooden spoon

1. Ask an adult to help you core the apples. Don't peel them, but chop them into bite-sized pieces.

2. Combine apples, broccoli and craisins in the salad bowl. Now you know your ABC's! Add walnuts and onion if you wish.

3. Add yogurt. Mix gently.

4. Time to eat!

If you don't have craisins, raisins will work, too.

Italian Flags (Caprese Salad)

Makes 5 servings • Prep Time: 15 minutes

INGREDIENTS

8 ounces balls of fresh part-skim mozzarella, about 15 balls

8 ounces grape or cherry tomatoes, about 10 tomatoes

10 large fresh basil leaves

10 fun party picks or any long toothpicks

Balsamic vinegar, *if you wish; not included in nutritional analysis*

EQUIPMENT

Cutting board

Knife

Kitchen towel

Serving platter

1. Ask an adult to help you cut each mozzarella ball in half. Set the balls aside. Then cut the tomatoes in half, too, and set them aside.

2. Hold the basil leaves under running water. Then gently pat them dry with the kitchen towel. Tear each leaf into 3 or 4 pieces.

3. Stick the sharp end of a pick through one basil leaf. Then add a tomato half to the pick. After that, add half a mozzarella ball.

4. Repeat by adding another tomato half, followed by another mozzarella half, and finish with one more tomato half.

5. Fill 9 more toothpicks in this way.

6. Eat as is or sprinkle a little vinegar on first.

Red and Green Salad With Chicken

FATS ●●○○○

Makes 4 main-dish servings • Prep Time: 45-60 minutes

INGREDIENTS

1 pound asparagus spears
 or snow peas

2 tablespoons water

¼ cup poppy seed dressing

1 tablespoon orange juice

8 cups torn fresh spinach,
 rinsed and patted dry

2 cups sliced fresh
 strawberries

¾ pound cooked *or* grilled
 chicken

¼ cup chopped pecans

EQUIPMENT

Cutting board

Knife

Microwave-safe glass bowl
 with lid

Potholders

Colander

Small bowl

Small whisk

Salad bowl

Kitchen shears

Wooden spoons or
 salad tongs

1. Break off the woody bottoms of the asparagus. Ask an adult to help you cut the spears into 1-inch pieces. If you're using snow peas instead, pinch off each pointy end and strip any strings off the sides.

2. Place vegetables and water in the glass bowl. Cover and microwave on high for 4-5 minutes, until the vegetables are a little soft.

3. Using potholders, remove the bowl from the microwave. Pour the vegetables into the colander in the sink. Run cold water over them right away. Allow them to drain.

4. In a small bowl, whisk together poppy-seed dressing and orange juice. Set the mixture aside.

5. Tear the spinach into bite-sized pieces and put in the salad bowl.

6. Ask an adult to help you slice the strawberries. Add them to the salad bowl.

7. Use the kitchen shears to cut the cooked chicken into bite-sized pieces. Add to the salad bowl.

8. Just before you're ready to eat, pour the dressing mixture over the salad. Using wooden spoons or salad tongs, toss gently so you don't smash the berries.

9. Sprinkle the pecans on top. Then serve.

Fiesta Chicken Salad

Makes 4 main-dish servings • Prep Time: 45 minutes

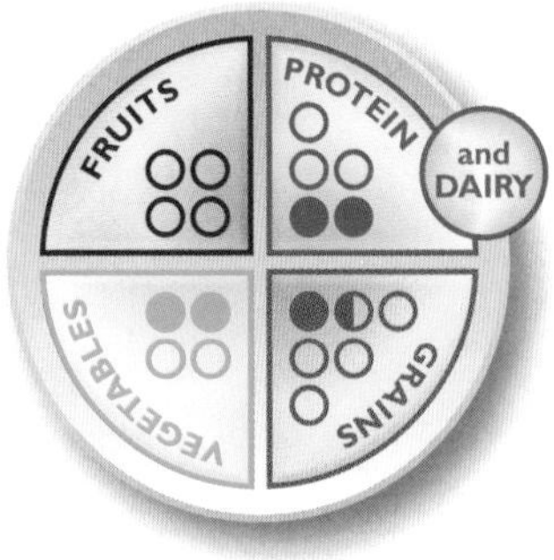

INGREDIENTS

1 head bibb lettuce, washed and patted dry

1 head red leaf lettuce, washed and patted dry

1 medium tomato

2 green onions

1 sweet red pepper, cored and seeded

1 cup shredded carrots

1 cup frozen corn, thawed and drained

1 pound cooked chicken (You can use canned or rotisserie chicken.)

1 teaspoon chili powder

½ cup shredded low-fat cheddar cheese

2 whole-wheat pita pockets, 4 inches in diameter

8 tablespoons fat-free ranch dressing

EQUIPMENT

Large bowl

Kitchen shears

Small bowl

Wooden spoon

1. Tear lettuce into bite-sized pieces and mix together in a large bowl.

2. Using the kitchen shears, snip tomato, green onions and red pepper into bite-sized pieces. Add to the salad bowl.

3. Top with shredded carrots and corn.

4. With the kitchen shears, snip chicken into bite-sized pieces. Put the pieces in a small bowl and toss with the chili powder. Lay gently on top of the salad.

5. Sprinkle the salad with cheese.

6. Use your fingers or the kitchen shears to divide each pita into 4 wedges. You will have 8 wedges.

7. Just before it's time to eat, add dressing and toss.

8. Serve with pita pockets.

41

Curly Pasta Salad

Makes 8 main-dish servings • Prep Time: 40 minutes
Cooking Time: 15 minutes

FATS ●●○○○

INGREDIENTS

14½-ounce box whole-wheat rotini

1 pint cherry tomatoes

1 medium red bell pepper

1 medium yellow bell pepper

1 medium cucumber

Half a red onion, *if you want; not included in nutritional analysis*

2 cups fresh broccoli florets

⅓ cup sliced black olives, *if you want; not included in nutritional analysis*

1 teaspoon salt-free Italian herb seasoning

¼ cup olive oil

½ cup red wine vinegar

8 teaspoons grated Parmesan cheese

EQUIPMENT

Large saucepan

Colander

Kitchen shears

Large bowl

Cutting board

Knife

Wooden spoon

Jar with a tight lid

1. Ask an adult to help you cook the pasta according to directions on the pasta box. But don't add salt to the water Put the hot, cooked pasta in a colander in the sink. Rinse with cool water. Let the pasta drain while you work on the vegetables.

2. Using the kitchen shears, snip tomatoes and peppers into bite-sized pieces. Place in the large bowl.

3. With an adult's help, thinly slice the cucumber. If you're using the onion, ask an adult to help you chop it up. Place cucumber and onion in the large bowl.

4. Add broccoli, and black olives if you wish, to the large bowl. Add cooled, drained pasta. Gently mix it all up.

5. Put seasoning, oil and vinegar in the jar. Make sure the lid is on tight! Shake well until the dressing is mixed.

6. When you're ready to serve, divide the pasta mixture between 8 plates. Top each with 1½ tablespoons of dressing and 1 teaspoon of grated Parmesan.

Since the dressing and cheese aren't mixed in with everything else, the pasta salad keeps longer so leftovers are good.

Silly Dilly Salad

Makes 10 servings • Prep Time: 1 hour
Cooking Time: 7-10 minutes • Chilling Time: 1 hour

FRUITS PROTEIN and DAIRY VEGETABLES GRAINS

FATS ●○○○○

INGREDIENTS

12-ounce package tricolor
 rotini pasta

1 cucumber

3 green onions

1 cup diced red bell pepper

1¼ cups frozen baby peas,
 thawed and drained

¼ cup fat-free mayonnaise

¾ cup plain fat-free yogurt

3 teaspoons dried dill weed

¼ teaspoon black pepper

⅔ cup fat-free feta cheese,
 crumbled

EQUIPMENT

Large saucepan with lid

Colander

Vegetable peeler

Cutting board

Knife

Kitchen shears

Salad bowl with lid or plastic
 wrap

Small bowl

Small whisk

Wooden spoon

1. Ask an adult to help you cook the pasta for 2 minutes **less** than the time given on the package. Immediately drain the pasta in the colander in the sink. Run cold water over the pasta. Let it drain and cool completely.

2. With the vegetable peeler, peel off 3 thin strips of peel down the whole length of the cucumber. Now your cucumber is striped! Ask an adult to help you cut the cucumber into thin rounds. Put them in the salad bowl.

3. Use the kitchen shears to snip the green onions into pieces. Snip the red pepper into small pieces, too. Place all these vegetables in the salad bowl.

4. Add the peas and the drained pasta to the bowl. Mix gently.

5. Now make the dressing. Put mayonnaise, yogurt, dill weed and pepper in the small bowl. Whisk together.

6. Pour the dressing over the pasta mixture. Mix again gently.

7. Cover the salad bowl with a lid or plastic wrap. Refrigerate at least 1 hour.

8. When you're ready to serve the salad, sprinkle feta cheese on top.

Taco in a Bowl

Makes 4 main-dish servings • Prep Time: 25 minutes
Cooking Time: 15 minutes

FATS ●○○○○

INGREDIENTS

⅓ cup diced green pepper

⅓ cup diced onion

2 tomatoes

2 cups torn lettuce

15-ounce can pinto, kidney
  or black beans, rinsed and
  drained

1 tablespoon canola oil

2 teaspoons taco seasoning
  mix

⅛ teaspoon pepper

EQUIPMENT

Kitchen shears

Knife

Cutting board

Safety can opener

Colander

Medium saucepan

Medium bowl

Potato masher

Soup bowls

1. Using the kitchen shears, snip the green pepper into small pieces. Ask an adult to help you dice the onion. Set both aside.

2. Use the kitchen shears to cut up the tomatoes. Rip or snip the lettuce into bite-sized pieces. Set both aside.

3. Open the can of beans. Pour beans into the colander in the sink. Run water through the beans until they are completely rinsed. Leave them in the strainer to drain.

4. Put the oil in the saucepan. With an adult's help, turn the heat to medium. Add the pepper and onion to the hot oil. Stir often and cook for about 5 minutes, until the pepper and onion are softened.

5. While the vegetables are cooking, put the drained beans in the medium bowl. Mash with the potato masher until all the beans are mashed up.

6. Add the mashed beans to the saucepan. Add the taco seasoning and pepper. With the heat on low, stir often and heat until bubbly hot.

7. To make a taco bowl, put some lettuce in a soup bowl. Dollop some bean mixture on top. Sprinkle chopped tomatoes on the very top.

8. Serve now!

To make the beans extra smooth, ask an adult to help you buzz them in a blender instead of mashing them in Step 5.

Tasty Tomato Soup

Makes 4 servings • Prep Time: 10 minutes
Cooking Time: 20 minutes

INGREDIENTS

2 tablespoons chopped onion

1 tablespoon olive oil

3 tablespoons flour

2 teaspoons sugar

¼ teaspoon pepper

¼ teaspoon dried basil

½ teaspoon dried oregano

¼ teaspoon dried thyme

4 cups canned pureed tomatoes,
   no salt added

2 cups skim milk

EQUIPMENT

Cutting board

Knife

Large saucepan

Wooden spoon

Safety can opener

1. With an adult helping you, chop the onion.

2. Ask an adult to help you turn the stove to medium. Pour the oil into the saucepan.

3. Put the onions in the pan. Cook and stir until they get soft, at least 5 minutes.

4. Add flour, sugar, pepper, basil, oregano and thyme. Stir.

5. Set the pan on the counter. Pour the tomatoes into the pan, with an adult helping you so you don't splash yourself. Stir everything together.

6. Put the pan back on the stove. Keep stirring until soup comes to a boil (when it really bubbles strongly).

7. Stop stirring. Let the soup boil for 1 minute.

8. Pour in the milk. Reduce heat to low and cook for 10 minutes, stirring often. Be careful not to let the soup boil after the milk is in it.

9. When the soup is hot, serve.

Always remember to pull out a trivet and put it on the countertop before you lift a hot pan off the stove. Then you're prepared to set the hot pan on it and won't hurt your counter or tabletop.

Garden-Patch Soup

Makes 6 servings • Prep Time: 30 minutes • Cooking Time: 30 minutes

FATS ◑○○○○

INGREDIENTS

1 onion

1 bell pepper

1 tablespoon olive oil

1 small zucchini, chopped

½ pound fresh mushrooms, cleaned

1 tablespoon chopped fresh basil leaves

24-ounce can tomatoes, no salt added, undrained

2 cups water

3 cubes reduced-sodium vegetable bouillon

2 cups whole-grain rotini

EQUIPMENT

Cutting board

Knife

Kitchen shears

Soup pot with lid

Large saucepan with lid

Wooden spoon

Timer

Safety can opener

Colander

1. Ask an adult to help you chop the onion. Use the kitchen shears to snip the bell pepper into small pieces.

2. Ask an adult to help you heat oil in the soup pot. Add onion and bell pepper to the hot oil. Stir now and then until they're tender, about 5 minutes.

3. Ask an adult to help you chop the zucchini. Add to the soup pot.

4. Ask an adult to help you slice the mushrooms and chop the basil leaves. Add these to the veggies, too.

5. Remove the pot from the heat. Carefully stir in tomatoes, water and bouillon cubes. Return to stove and cook over medium heat.

6. When the soup starts boiling (bubbling), put the lid on the pot. Set a timer for 10 minutes.

7. Meanwhile, ask an adult to help you cook the rotini in the saucepan. Follow the directions on the rotini box. Don't add salt to the water. Drain the cooked pasta in the colander.

8. When the timer goes off, remove the pot with the vegetables from the heat. Add the cooked rotini to the soup with an adult's help. Stir.

9. Now it's time to eat.

Quick-Fix Veggie Soup

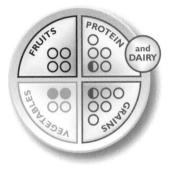

Makes 8 servings • Prep Time: 30 minutes
Cooking Time: 35-40 minutes

INGREDIENTS

½ cup chopped onion

14½-ounce can diced tomatoes, undrained, no salt added

½ pound extra-lean ground beef

1 teaspoon olive oil

¾ cup uncooked quick-cooking barley

5 cups water

2 cubes low-sodium beef bouillon

1 teaspoon minced garlic

½ teaspoon crushed dried basil

½ cup frozen sliced carrots

9-ounce package frozen mixed vegetables

EQUIPMENT

Knife

Cutting board

Safety can opener

Microwave-safe glass bowl with lid

Potholders

Wooden spoon

Colander

Medium bowl

Large saucepan with lid

1. With an adult helping you, chop the onion. Set it aside.

2. Open the can of tomatoes. Set it aside.

3. Put the ground beef in the glass bowl. Cover and microwave on high 5 minutes.

4. With potholders, take the bowl out of the microwave. Lift the lid, keeping your face and hands away from the steam. Break up the meat with a wooden spoon. If it's still pink in parts, put it back in the microwave to cook on high for another minute.

5. Check the meat again. Do this until the meat is browned the whole way through.

6. Set the colander over a medium bowl. Ask an adult to help you carefully spoon the beef into the colander. The fat will drip down into the bowl.

7. With an adult's help, heat oil over medium heat in the saucepan. Add the onion. Stir and cook until the onion is getting soft, at least 5 minutes.

8. Add cooked beef, tomatoes, barley, water, bouillon cubes, garlic and dried basil. Stir.

9. Put the lid on and turn the heat up. When the soup is boiling (bubbling with strength), turn the heat down so the soup is simmering, a very low boil. Simmer for 10 minutes, asking an adult to help you stir it occasionally.

10. Stir in the frozen vegetables. Cook 10 more minutes on low. If the soup is too thick for your liking, add a little water and stir again. When it's hot the whole way through, the soup is ready to serve.

Cheesy Corn Soup

Makes 6 servings • Prep Time: 30 minutes
Cooking Time: 25-30 minutes

INGREDIENTS

2 cups unpeeled diced potatoes

1 cup diced carrots

1 cup chopped celery

½ cup water

½ teaspoon salt

¼ teaspoon pepper

2 cups cream-style corn

1½ cups skim milk

⅔ cup grated low-fat cheddar cheese

EQUIPMENT

Cutting board

Knife

Large soup pot with lid

Wooden spoon

1. With an adult helping you, cut the potatoes into little cubes. Put them into the soup pot.

2. Also have an adult help you cut up the carrots and the celery. Add them to the soup pot.

3. Add water, salt and pepper to the soup pot. Put the lid on.

4. With an adult's help, turn the heat on the stove to medium. Bring soup to a boil (when the water bubbles vigorously).

5. Then turn the heat to low. Keep the pot covered and let the vegetables simmer (a slow bubble) for 10 minutes.

6. Add corn. Stir. Cover and simmer 5 more minutes.

7. Remove the pot from the stove. Add milk and cheese.

8. Return the pot to the stove. With an adult helping you, stir until the cheese melts and the soup is hot the whole way through. Cook slowly so the soup doesn't boil now that you've added the cheese and milk.

9. Dip into individual soup bowls and serve.

Cowboy Chili

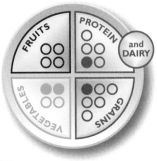

Makes 8 servings • Prep Time: 15 minutes
Cooking Time: 15-20 minutes

INGREDIENTS

15-ounce can black beans, no salt added

15-ounce can garbanzo beans, no salt added

15-ounce can kidney beans, no salt added

½ cup water

1 cup salsa, mild or spicy

Two 8-ounce cans tomato sauce, no salt added

1 tablespoon chili powder

Low-fat sour cream, *if you wish; not included in nutritional analysis*

Reduced-fat cheddar cheese, grated, *if you wish; not included in nutritional analysis*

EQUIPMENT

Safety can opener

Colander

Medium bowl

Fork or potato masher

Large saucepan with lid

Wooden spoon

1. Open the can of black beans. Pour the beans in the colander in the sink. Run water over the beans to rinse them off.

2. Pour the rinsed beans into the medium bowl. Use the fork or potato masher to mash them up completely. Scrape the mashed beans into the saucepan.

3. Open the garbanzo beans and kidney beans and rinse them, but don't mash them. Put the beans in the saucepan.

4. Add water, salsa, tomato sauce and chili powder. Mix well.

5. Put the lid on the saucepan. With an adult's help, turn the heat to medium.

6. Cook over medium heat about 10 minutes, stirring occasionally. The chili should be gently bubbling and hot.

7. Scoop chili into serving bowls. Serve with sour cream and grated cheese for people to put on their chili if they wish.

Beans are high in protein and can stand in for meat. That's why this recipe counts as a Protein/Dairy serving.

Asian Green Beans

FATS ◑○○○○

Makes 6 servings • Prep Time: 10 minutes
Cooking Time: 10 minutes

INGREDIENTS

¾ pound fresh green beans,
washed

1 tablespoon low-sodium
soy sauce

2 teaspoons minced garlic

1 teaspoon brown sugar

1 teaspoon peanut butter

1 tablespoon sesame seeds

1 tablespoon canola oil

EQUIPMENT

Small bowl

Small whisk

Large skillet

Wooden spoon

Serving bowl

1. Pinch off the ends of the green beans.
Break each bean in two. Set them aside.

2. In the small bowl, whisk together soy sauce, garlic,
brown sugar and peanut butter. Set aside.

3. Put sesame seeds in the skillet. Ask an adult to help you
stir them over medium heat for a few minutes until they
begin to smell toasted. Take off the heat right away and pour
sesame seeds into the serving bowl.

4. Ask an adult to help you heat oil in the skillet. Stir-fry the
green beans with the wooden spoon until they're tender-
crisp, about 5-7 minutes. Keep stirring the whole time.

5. Then put the beans in the serving bowl on top of the
sesame seeds.

6. Pour the peanut butter sauce on top. Mix until all of the
green beans are coated with the sauce and the seeds.

7. Call everyone to the table!

Alert!
Some of your family and
friends may have a peanut
allergy. If that's the case,
leave out the peanut butter
when making this recipe.

Succotash

Makes 6 servings • Prep Time: 10 minutes
Cooking Time: 10-12 minutes

FATS ●○○○○

INGREDIENTS

2 slices low-sodium
 Canadian bacon

2 cups frozen shelled
 edamame (soybeans),
 thawed

2 cups frozen corn, thawed

¼ cup low-fat, low-sodium
 chicken broth

EQUIPMENT

Knife

Cutting board

Medium saucepan with lid

Wooden spoon

1. With an adult helping you, chop the Canadian bacon into small pieces. Put the pieces into the saucepan.

2. Add edamame, corn and broth to the saucepan. Stir. Put on the lid.

3. With an adult's help, cook over medium heat for 5-10 minutes, until the mixture is steaming. If you like softer vegetables, cook a few minutes longer.

4. It's ready to serve!

"Succotash" is a Native American word for a one-pot meal they used to make. When the Europeans made this dish, they seasoned it with bear fat!

Creamy Corn and Broccoli Bake

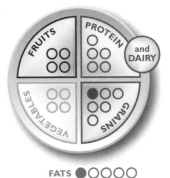

FATS ●○○○○

Makes 6 servings • Prep Time: 10 minutes • Cooking Time: 45 minutes

INGREDIENTS

½ cup crushed unsalted soda crackers, *divided*

16-ounce can cream-style corn, no salt added

16-ounce package frozen chopped broccoli, thawed

1 egg, beaten

⅛ teaspoon pepper

1 tablespoon trans-fat-free margarine, at room temperature

EQUIPMENT

Cooking spray

1½-quart casserole dish

Plastic bag

Rolling pin

Mixing bowl

Safety can opener

Wooden spoon

Small bowl

Potholders

1. Preheat the oven to 350° F. Spray the casserole dish with cooking spray.

2. To crush the crackers, put them in the plastic bag. Roll the bag with the rolling pin until the crackers are in fine crumbs. Put ¼ cup of the cracker crumbs in the mixing bowl. (Keep the rest in the plastic bag until you need them.)

3. Open the can of corn. Add it to the mixing bowl.

4. Add the broccoli, egg and pepper. Mix everything up.

5. Spoon the corn mixture into the casserole dish. Smooth out the top with the spoon.

6. In a small bowl, mix together the margarine and the remaining crushed crackers. Sprinkle on top of the filled casserole dish.

7. With an adult's help, put the dish in the oven. Bake for 45 minutes. With an adult helping you, and using potholders, take the casserole out of the oven.

8. Cut into 6 pieces and serve.

Before you take the hot casserole dish out of the oven, find a trivet to put it on so it doesn't burn your counter or tabletop.

Honey Carrots

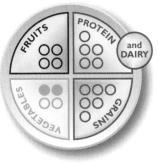

Makes 4 servings • Prep Time: 10 minutes
Cooking Time: 10-15 minutes

FATS ⬤◯◯◯◯

INGREDIENTS

16-ounce package baby
    carrots

¼ cup water

2 teaspoons olive oil

1 tablespoon honey *or*
    agave nectar

2 teaspoons lemon juice

EQUIPMENT

Large microwave-safe
    glass bowl with lid
    or plastic wrap

Potholders

Fork

Wooden spoon

Small microwave-safe
    glass bowl

Colander

1. Put carrots and water in the large glass bowl. Cover it either with its lid or with plastic wrap.

2. Microwave on high for 3 minutes. Using potholders, take the bowl out of the microwave. Carefully lift the lid, keeping your face and hands away from the steam. Poke the carrots with a fork to see if they're as tender as you like. If not, cover and microwave on high for 1 more minute. Check again.

3. Meanwhile, combine olive oil, honey and lemon juice in the small bowl.

4. When the carrots are as tender as you like them, set them aside. Put the honey mixture in the microwave on high for 20-30 seconds. Take the bowl out with potholders. Stir the sauce.

5. With an adult's help, pour the carrots into the colander to drain off the water. Pour the honey glaze over the carrots and mix everything together.

6. Time to serve.

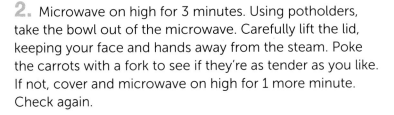

Children younger than 1 year old shouldn't eat honey. Use agave nectar instead if a baby might be eating some of this recipe.

Italian Oven Fries

Makes 6 servings • Prep Time: 30 minutes • Cooking Time: 30 minutes

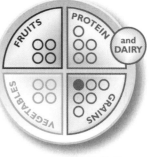

INGREDIENTS

2 tablespoons grated Parmesan cheese

2 teaspoons olive oil

1 tablespoon dried basil

½ teaspoon dried oregano

¼ teaspoon garlic powder

4 medium red potatoes

EQUIPMENT

Jellyroll baking pan

Cooking spray

Large mixing bowl

Wooden spoon

Cutting board

Knife

Metal spatula

Potholders

1. Preheat the oven to 450° F. Spray the pan with cooking spray.

FATS ●○○○○

2. Put Parmesan cheese, olive oil, basil, oregano and garlic powder in the mixing bowl. Mix together well.

3. Ask an adult to help you cut the potatoes into wedges.

4. Add the potato wedges to the cheese mixture. Mix gently until all the potato wedges are coated.

5. Put the coated potato wedges on the pan. Spread in a single layer.

6. With an adult helping you, put the pan in the oven. Bake for 15 minutes.

7. With an adult helping you, and using the potholders, remove the pan from the oven. Flip and stir the fries with the metal spatula.

8. With an adult helping you, put the pan back in the oven to bake for 15 more minutes. The oven fries should be crispy on the outside and tender inside — and yummy!

9. Eat right away.

Mashed Potato Hills

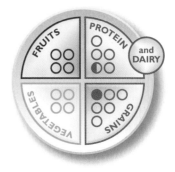

Makes 8 servings • Prep Time: 50 minutes
Cooking Time: 40-45 minutes

INGREDIENTS

2 pounds Yukon Gold
  potatoes

2 cubes reduced-sodium
  chicken bouillon

Water

¼ cup skim milk

4 ounces fat-free cream
  cheese, at room
  temperature (use half
  of an 8-ounce package)
  and cut into cubes

¼ cup fat-free sour cream

½ cup low-fat shredded
  sharp cheddar cheese

2 teaspoons chopped
  fresh parsley

EQUIPMENT

Baking sheet

Cooking spray

Vegetable peeler

Cutting board

Knife

Medium saucepan
  with lid

Fork

Potato masher

Wooden spoon

Potholders

Kitchen shears

1. Preheat the oven to 450° F. Spray the baking sheet with cooking spray.

2. With an adult helping you, peel the potatoes and cut them into small cubes. You can skip peeling the potatoes if you want.

3. Place potatoes in the saucepan. Put bouillon cubes in the pan with the potatoes. Add water until it barely covers the potatoes. Put the lid on.

4. With an adult helping you, turn the heat to medium. Cook until the water begins to boil (bubble vigorously).

5. Cook for about 30 minutes, or until the potatoes are very soft when you poke them with a fork.

6. With an adult's help, drain the potatoes. Put them back in the pan. Mash them with the potato masher.

7. Add milk, cream cheese, sour cream and cheddar cheese to potatoes. Mix well.

8. Scoop the mashed potatoes into 6 hills on the baking sheet.

9. Smooth the hills into ovals, using the wooden spoon.

10. With an adult helping you, put the baking sheet in the oven. Bake for 10-15 minutes, or until the hills are golden brown.

11. While the hills are baking, snip the parsley into little pieces using the kitchen shears.

12. With an adult's help, and using potholders, take the baking sheet out of the oven.

13. Sprinkle the hills with the chopped parsley and serve.

Sweet Potato Mashup

Makes 6 servings • Prep Time: 40 minutes
Cooking Time: 40-45 minutes

INGREDIENTS

1 cup cooked *or* canned sweet potatoes

1 very ripe medium banana

1 cup evaporated skim milk

1 tablespoon brown sugar

½ cup egg substitute, beaten

¼ teaspoon salt

¼ cup raisins

1 tablespoon honey *or* agave nectar

1 teaspoon ground cinnamon

EQUIPMENT

1-quart baking dish

Cooking spray

Medium mixing bowl

Potato masher

Safety can opener

Wooden spoon

Small bowl

Table knife

1. Preheat the oven to 325° F. Spray the baking dish with cooking spray.

2. In the medium bowl, mash the sweet potato and the banana together with the potato masher.

3. Add evaporated milk. Mix well.

4. Add brown sugar, egg substitute and salt. Mix well with the wooden spoon.

5. Pour the sweet potato mixture into the baking dish.

6. In a small bowl, mix together raisins, honey and cinnamon. Sprinkle over top of the sweet potato mixture.

Children younger than 1 year old shouldn't eat honey. Use agave nectar instead if a baby might be eating some of this recipe.

7. With an adult helping you, put the baking dish into the oven. Bake for 40-45 minutes.

8. Ask an adult to help you take the casserole out of the oven. Stick a table knife in the center of the potatoes. If there's gooey stuff on the knife when you pull it out, bake the casserole a few more minutes. Then check it again. It's done when the knife comes out clean.

9. Call everyone to come and eat.

Don't throw bananas away that are squishy with really dark skins! They're perfect for this dish.

Cheesy Zucchini Caterpillar

Makes 2 servings • Prep Time: 20 minutes
Cooking Time: 35-40 minutes

FATS ●○○○○

INGREDIENTS

1 medium zucchini,
   about 6 inches long

1 teaspoon olive oil

⅛ teaspoon garlic powder

⅛ teaspoon onion
   powder

2 tablespoons grated
   Parmesan cheese

EQUIPMENT

Cutting board

Knife

Paper towel

Aluminum foil

Baking sheet

Fork

Potholders

1. Preheat the oven to 375° F.

2. Ask an adult to help you trim the ends off the zucchini. At every half inch along the zucchini, slice most of the way through the zucchini, but don't cut all the way down. It should look like the zucchini is sliced in rounds, but all the slices are still connected underneath.

3. Gently pat the zucchini dry with a paper towel.

4. Place the zucchini on a piece of aluminum foil large enough to wrap completely around it.

5. Drizzle the top of the zucchini with olive oil.

6. Sprinkle with garlic and onion powders.

7. Wrap the zucchini in foil and pinch closed. Lay it on the baking sheet.

8. Ask an adult to help you put the baking sheet in the oven. Bake for 30-35 minutes, or until the zucchini is tender when you poke it with a fork.

9. Pick up your potholders, and ask an adult to help you take the baking sheet out of the oven.

10. Using the potholders, open the foil, keeping away from the steam. Sprinkle the cheese over the zucchini. Leave the foil open.

11. Ask an adult to help you put the zucchini back in the oven for 1-2 minutes, until the cheese melts and turns a little brown.

12. Eat warm.

Salsa Rice

Makes 6 servings • Prep Time: 15 minutes
Cooking Time: 35-45 minutes

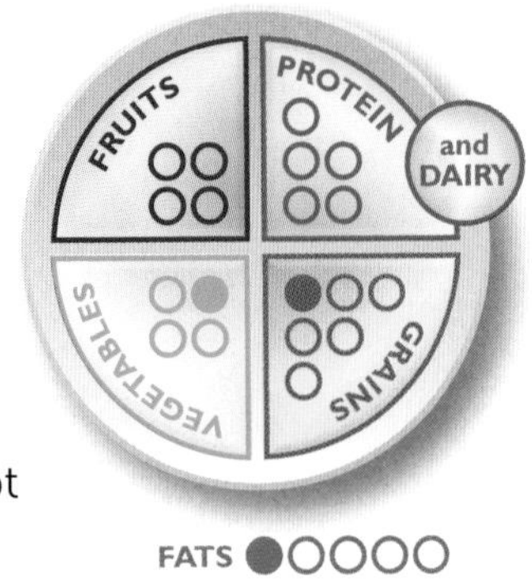

FATS ●○○○○

INGREDIENTS

1 tablespoon olive oil

½ cup low-sodium tomato juice

1½ cups water

½ cup salsa, mild or spicy

¼ teaspoon cumin

¼ teaspoon chili powder

½ teaspoon garlic powder

½ teaspoon minced onion

1 tablespoon brown sugar

1 cup uncooked long-grain rice

EQUIPMENT

Large saucepan with lid

Wooden spoon

1. Put all the ingredients — except the rice — in a large saucepan. Put the lid on.

2. With an adult helping you, turn the heat on the stove to medium and bring the mixture to a boil. (It will be bubbling vigorously.)

3. With an adult's help, remove the pan from the heat. Lift the lid and stir the mixture. Add the rice. Stir again.

4. Put the lid back on. Put the pan back on the stove. Turn the heat to low. Cook for 20 minutes.

5. With an adult nearby, lift the lid and see if the liquids are gone. If they're not, put the lid back on and cook for another 5 minutes. Check again. Keep cooking and checking until the liquid is gone. Turn off the heat and serve.

When the liquids have disappeared in Step 5, the rice has totally soaked them up and gotten nice and tender and flavorful.

Wild West Pasta
Page 86

Quesadillas
Page 90

Mama Mia
Veggie Pizza
Page 78

Shrimp and Pasta
Page 82

Blueberry French Toast
Page 92

Chapter 3
Great Grains

Mama Mia Veggie Pizza

FATS ●○○○○

Makes 12-15 inch pizza, 6 servings   •   Prep Time: 30 minutes
Cooking Time: 15-20 minutes

INGREDIENTS

One 12-15 inch refrigerated whole-wheat pizza crust

¾ cup spaghetti *or* pizza sauce

1 teaspoon salt-free Italian herb seasoning, *divided*

¾ cup grated low-sodium, low-fat mozzarella cheese

Pick 3 or more vegetables for toppings from this list:

1 small onion, chopped

1 large bell pepper, chopped

¼ cup green *or* black olives, sliced

1½ cups sliced fresh mushrooms

1 cup broccoli florets

1 medium zucchini, sliced

1 tomato, sliced

EQUIPMENT

Baking stone or cookie sheet

Spatula

Kitchen shears

Potholders

Pizza cutter

1. Lay the crust on a baking stone or cookie sheet. Check the crust wrapper for baking temperature and time. Preheat the oven.

2. Use the spatula to evenly spread the spaghetti sauce on the crust. Sprinkle with ½ teaspoon Italian herb seasoning.

3. Sprinkle the cheese evenly over the sauce.

4. Did you and an adult pick 3 vegetable toppings and prepare them? Use the kitchen shears to snip your veggie toppings into bite-sized pieces.

5. Sprinkle the vegetables evenly over the cheese. Sprinkle with the remaining herb mix.

6. With an adult's help, put the pizza in the hot oven. Bake according to the time and temperature on the crust wrapper.

7. With an adult's help, and using potholders, remove the finished pizza from the oven. Cut into 6 wedges and serve.

Pasta Primo

Makes 6 main-dish servings • Prep Time: 40-60 minutes
Cooking Time: 25 minutes

INGREDIENTS

3 cups broccoli florets

2 small zucchini, sliced into ¼-inch-thick
  rounds

1 red bell pepper, cut in strips or chunks

2 cups (1 pint) grape tomatoes

1-2 teaspoons minced garlic, *if you like;
  not included in nutritional analysis*

8-ounce package whole-grain fettuccine

1 teaspoon olive oil

Sauce:

  ¾ cup skim milk

  1 tablespoon olive oil

  ⅔ cup part-skim ricotta cheese

  ¼ cup grated reduced-fat Parmesan cheese

  2 tablespoons chopped fresh basil *or*
    1 tablespoon dried basil

EQUIPMENT

Cutting board

Knife

Large microwave-safe glass bowl with lid
  or plastic wrap

Kitchen shears

Potholders

Wooden spoon

Large saucepan with lid

Colander

Blender

Medium microwave-safe glass bowl

Large serving bowl

FATS ●○○○○

1. Ask an adult to help you cut up the broccoli and zucchini with a knife. Put them in the large glass bowl.

2. Using the kitchen shears, cut the pepper into strips or chunks. Add these to the glass bowl.

3. Cover the bowl and microwave on high for 2 minutes.

4. Using potholders, ask an adult to help you remove the bowl from the microwave. Carefully lift the lid or wrap, keeping your face and hands away from any steam. Stir.

5. Cover again and microwave for 1 more minute. Using potholders, remove the bowl.

6. Cut the tomatoes in half with the kitchen shears, or ask an adult to cut the tomatoes for you.

7. Toss the tomatoes into the bowl. Add the garlic now, if you wish. Cover again. Set aside. (The heat will steam the tomatoes and garlic, so there's no need to microwave them.)

8. With an adult helping you, cook the fettuccine according to the directions on the box. But don't add salt to the pasta water.

9. With an adult helping you, drain the cooked pasta in the colander. Return the pasta to the saucepan. Put the lid on to keep it warm.

10. While the pasta cooks, you can make the sauce. Put milk, oil, ricotta cheese, Parmesan cheese and basil in the blender. Put the lid on.

11. With an adult nearby, turn on the blender and watch until the liquid turns smooth. Pour the sauce into the medium glass bowl.

12. Microwave the sauce on high for 1-2 minutes, uncovered. Remove with potholders. Stir. If you want the sauce hotter, microwave again for 1-2 minutes.

13. Pour pasta, vegetables and sauce into the large serving bowl. Mix together gently and serve.

Shrimp and Pasta

Makes 6 main-dish servings • Prep Time: 30 minutes
Cooking Time: 25-30 minutes

INGREDIENTS

8 ounces whole-wheat angel hair pasta

12 fresh basil leaves, snipped

8 cherry tomatoes

1 pound cooked, peeled shrimp

1-3 cloves garlic, minced, *if you wish; not included in nutritional analysis*

⅛ teaspoon pepper, *if you wish; not included in nutritional analysis*

1 tablespoon olive oil

EQUIPMENT

Large saucepan with lid

Kitchen shears

Mixing bowl

Cutting board

Knife

Colander

Wooden spoon

1. With an adult helping you, cook the pasta according to the directions on the box. But don't add salt to the water.

2. Meanwhile, use the kitchen shears to snip the basil into pieces. Put it in the mixing bowl.

3. Ask an adult to help you cut the tomatoes in half. Add them to the mixing bowl.

4. Add the shrimp to the bowl. If you wish, add garlic and pepper to the bowl, too. Mix gently.

5. As soon as the pasta is done cooking, ask an adult to help you drain it in the colander. Put the drained pasta back in the saucepan. Mix in the oil.

6. Add the tomato and shrimp mixture to the hot pasta. Mix gently and thoroughly. Serve immediately.

Spaghetti Pie

Makes 4 servings • Prep Time: 30 minutes
Cooking Time: 45 minutes

INGREDIENTS

4 ounces thin whole-wheat spaghetti

1 tablespoon olive oil

2 tablespoons reduced-fat Parmesan cheese

Egg substitute equivalent to 1 egg

½ cup fat-free ricotta cheese

½ cup diced onion

½ cup diced green *or* red bell pepper

½ pound lean ground turkey

1 cup canned chopped tomatoes, no salt added, undrained

¼ cup tomato paste, no salt added

½ teaspoon dried basil

½ teaspoon dried oregano

¼ cup shredded low-fat mozzarella cheese

EQUIPMENT

8-inch glass pie plate

Cooking spray

Saucepan with lid

Colander

Wooden spoon

Cutting board

Knife

Safety can opener

Potholders

1. Preheat oven to 350° F. Spray the pie plate with cooking spray.

2. With an adult's help, cook the spaghetti according to directions on the box. But don't add salt to the water. Drain. Return to saucepan (off the stove).

3. Stir the oil, Parmesan cheese and beaten egg substitute into cooked spaghetti. Mix well.

4. Spoon the spaghetti mixture into the pie plate. Using your fingers or a spoon, spread the mixture over the bottom and up the sides to form a crust.

5. With a wooden spoon, spread the ricotta cheese over the bottom of the crust. Set aside.

6. With an adult helping you, dice the onion and the peppers.

7. Put onion, peppers and turkey in the saucepan. Ask an adult to help you turn the heat on the stove to medium. Stir and cook until the turkey is no longer pink. You may need to add a little water to the pan to prevent sticking.

8. Use the safety can opener to open the tomatoes and tomato paste. Measure the tomato paste.

9. Now add tomatoes, tomato paste, basil and oregano to pan. Cook for several minutes until steam rises and everything is heated through.

10. Carefully spoon the turkey and tomato mixture over the ricotta cheese.

11. With an adult helping you, put the spaghetti pie in the oven. Bake for 20 minutes.

12. With an adult helping you, and using potholders, take the pie out of the oven. Sprinkle the mozzarella cheese on top.

13. With an adult helping you again, and using potholders, put the pie back in the oven for 5 more minutes to melt the cheese.

14. Cut into wedges and serve.

Wild West Pasta

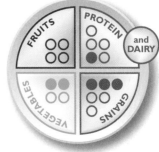

Makes 8 servings • Prep Time: 20 minutes
Cooking Time: 80-90 minutes

INGREDIENTS

1½ cups chopped onion

3 garlic cloves, minced

2 teaspoons olive oil

1 pound extra-lean ground beef

1 teaspoon black pepper

1 teaspoon dried oregano

½ teaspoon dried basil

28-ounce can tomato puree,
   no salt added

15-ounce can tomato sauce,
   no salt added

½ teaspoon sugar, *if you wish;
   not included in nutritional
   analysis*

1 pound wagon-wheel
   whole-wheat pasta

EQUIPMENT

Cutting board

Knife

Large stockpot with lid

Wooden spoon

Timer

Safety can opener

Medium stockpot

Colander

Serving bowl

1. Ask an adult to help you chop the onion and mince the garlic. Keep them separate. Set both aside.

2. Ask an adult to help you heat the oil in a large stockpot over medium heat. Stir in the onion and the ground beef.

3. Cook for about 10 minutes, breaking up the clumps of ground beef with the spoon. The beef is done when it is browned and no longer pink.

4. Add garlic, black pepper, oregano, basil, tomato puree and tomato sauce to the large stockpot. Add sugar, if you wish. Stir.

5. Turn the heat down to low. Rest the lid on top of the pot so the pot is not completely covered.

6. Cook over low heat for 80 minutes, stirring occasionally. So you don't forget: Set a timer for 20 minutes and stir — do that 4 times total.

7. With an adult's help, cook the pasta in the medium stockpot, following the directions on the pasta box. But don't add salt to the water. Drain the cooked pasta in the colander.

8. Place the drained pasta in the serving bowl. Top with the hot tomato sauce.

9. Call everyone to the table.

Chili Mac

Makes 10 servings • Prep Time: 30 minutes
Cooking Time: 35 minutes

INGREDIENTS

1 onion

1 pound whole-wheat macaroni

2 teaspoons olive oil

1 tablespoon chili powder

½ teaspoon cumin

¼ teaspoon garlic powder

15-ounce can diced tomatoes,
   no salt added

15-ounce can kidney beans,
   no salt added

15-ounce can sliced carrots,
   no salt added

¼ cup grated Parmesan cheese,
   divided

EQUIPMENT

Cutting board

Knife

Large saucepan with lid

Colander

Medium saucepan with lid

Safety can opener

Wooden spoon

Large serving bowl

1. Ask an adult to help you chop the onion. Set aside.

2. Ask an adult to help you prepare the macaroni in the large saucepan by following the directions on the macaroni box. But don't add salt to the water. Drain in colander. Rinse with cold water to keep it from sticking together. Set aside.

3. With an adult's help, heat oil in the medium saucepan. Add onion, chili powder, cumin and garlic powder. Stir and cook over medium heat until onion gets soft, at least 5 minutes.

4. Using the safety can opener, open the cans of tomatoes, beans and carrots. Pour beans and carrots into the colander in the sink. Run water over them. Do not drain the tomatoes.

5. Pour the can of tomatoes into the saucepan on top of the onion. Stir. Add the drained beans and carrots. Stir again.

6. Put the lid on the pan. Turn the heat to low. Cook the vegetable mixture until it's steaming and hot, about 5-10 minutes.

7. To serve, put cooked macaroni in a big serving bowl and spoon some bean mixture over it. Sprinkle with 1 teaspoon of grated Parmesan and stir. Then add more bean mixture and Parmesan to the bowl and stir. Continue doing this until you've used all of the bean mixture and the cheese.

8. Time to eat!

89

Quesadillas

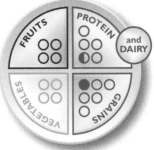

Makes 16 servings (a serving is 2 pieces)   •   Prep Time: 15 minutes
Cooking Time: 10-15 minutes

INGREDIENTS

Half a small onion, *if you like; not included in nutritional analysis*

4-ounce can diced green chili peppers, drained

¼ teaspoon ground cumin

8 fat-free white *or* whole wheat flour tortillas, 10 inches in diameter

2 cups (about 8 ounces) shredded reduced-fat Monterey Jack cheese

Salsa, mild or spicy

EQUIPMENT

Baking sheet

Cooking spray

Cutting board

Knife

Small bowl

Safety can opener

Wooden spoon

Potholders

Cooling rack

Kitchen shears

1. Preheat oven to 350° F. Lightly spray the baking sheet with cooking spray.

2. If you're using onion, ask an adult to help you chop it.

3. In the bowl combine chili peppers and cumin. Add onion if you want to use it. Set bowl aside.

4. Put the tortillas on the baking sheet. Sprinkle half of each tortilla with ¼ cup cheese.

5. Divide the chili pepper mixture among the tortillas as evenly as you can, spreading it over the cheese side, not the bare side.

6. Fold the bare side of each tortilla over the filled side so you have eight half-moon shapes.

7. With an adult helping you, put the baking sheet in the oven. Bake for 10-15 minutes, or until the cheese melts.

8. Ask an adult to help you, and using potholders, take the pan out of the oven. Set it on a cooling rack.

9. Using the kitchen shears and potholders, snip each quesadilla in half and then in half again. You'll have 4 pieces from each quesadilla. Serve with your favorite salsa for dipping.

Blueberry French Toast

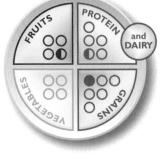

Makes 9 servings • Prep Time: 15 minutes
Chilling Time: 8 hours or overnight • Cooking Time: 15-20 minutes

INGREDIENTS

12-inch French baguette, preferably whole-wheat

½ cup egg substitute

1 cup fat-free soy milk *or* skim *or* low-fat milk

¼ teaspoon nutmeg

¼ teaspoon cinnamon

1 teaspoon vanilla

4 tablespoons brown sugar, *divided*

¾ cup blueberries

1 tablespoon canola oil

EQUIPMENT

Cooking spray

9-inch square baking pan

Cutting board

Knife

Large bowl

Whisk

Plastic wrap

Small bowl

Wooden spoon

Potholders

Cooling rack

1. Spray the baking dish with cooking spray. Set it aside.

2. With an adult helping you, cut the baguette into 10 slices, each 1 inch thick. Lay the slices in a single layer in the baking dish.

Baguettes are long sticks of French bread.

3. In a large bowl, whisk the egg substitute until frothy.

4. Whisk in milk, nutmeg, cinnamon, vanilla and 2 tablespoons brown sugar.

5. Pour this mixture evenly over bread. Then turn each slice over so it is coated on both sides.

6. Cover the pan with plastic wrap. Stick it in the refrigerator for at least 8 hours or overnight. During that time, the bread will absorb the liquid.

7. When you're ready to bake, preheat oven to 450° F.

8. Drop the blueberries evenly over the bread slices.

9. In a small bowl, stir together the remaining 2 tablespoons of brown sugar and the oil. Spoon this mixture evenly over the bread.

10. With an adult helping you, put the pan in the oven. Bake uncovered for about 20 minutes, or until the liquid from the blueberries is bubbling. Using potholders, take the pan out of the oven.

11. Set the pan on the cooling rack until you're ready to serve.

Sizzlin' Chicken Fajitas
Page 108

Yummy
Chicken Noodle Soup
Page 100

Tuna Flippers
Page 102

Eggs a Go-Go
Page 96

Crispy Chicken Fingers
Page 106

Chapter 4

Plenty of Protein
(also known as poultry, fish, meat, eggs and dairy)

Eggs a Go-Go

Makes 3 main-dish servings (a serving is 4 muffin cups)
Prep Time: 30 minutes   •   Cooking Time: 20-25 minutes

INGREDIENTS

16-ounce package frozen chopped spinach

¼ cup diced green bell sweet peppers *or* finely chopped broccoli florets

¼ cup diced onion

2 cups (16 ounces) liquid egg substitute

¾ cup shredded reduced-fat mozzarella cheese

EQUIPMENT

12-cup muffin pan or two 6-cup pans

12 foil baking cups

Cooking spray

Glass bowl

Potholders

Medium mixing bowl

Kitchen shears

Cutting board

Knife

Whisk

Table knife

1. Preheat oven to 350° F.
Put the foil cups in the muffin pan.
Spray each cup with cooking spray.

2. Unwrap the spinach and place in the glass bowl. Microwave on high for 2½ minutes. Use potholders to remove the bowl from the microwave. Set aside to cool.

3. When the spinach is cool enough to handle, pick up a handful. Squeeze out the liquid over the sink. Put the spinach in the medium mixing bowl. Repeat until all the spinach is squeezed dry and has been added to the bowl.

4. Use the kitchen shears to snip up the bell peppers. If you're using broccoli, ask an adult to help you chop it. Make the pieces slightly smaller than bite-sized. Add to the mixing bowl.

5. Ask an adult to help you chop the onion. Add to the bowl.

6. Add egg substitute and cheese to the bowl.

7. Mix everything with the whisk.

8. Using a measuring cup, put ¼ cup of the mixture in each foil cup. If there's extra, divide it evenly among the cups. Each foil cup should have almost the same amount.

9. Have an adult help you to put the muffin pan in the oven. Bake for 20 minutes.

10. Stick a table knife blade into the centers of several muffins. If nothing sticks to the knife when you pull it out, the eggs are done. If the knife isn't clean, continue baking another 3 minutes. Test with a knife again. Serve when fully cooked.

Big Baked Eggs

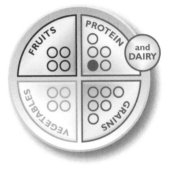

Makes 4 servings • Prep Time: 15 minutes
Cooking Time: 10-15 minutes

INGREDIENTS

4 tablespoons grated Parmesan *or* Asiago cheese, *divided*

4 jumbo eggs

Freshly ground pepper, *if you like*

4 tablespoons skim milk, *divided*

EQUIPMENT

4- or 6-cup muffin pan

Cooking spray

Grater

Potholders

Table knife

Fork

1. Preheat the oven to 350° F. Spray 4 cups in the muffin pan with cooking spray.

2. Grate the cheese. Set aside.

3. Carefully break an egg into each of the 4 greased cups. (Try not to break the yolk, but if you do, it's not a problem.) Sprinkle with pepper, if you like.

4. Add 1 tablespoon milk to each cup.

5. Top each with 1 tablespoon grated cheese.

6. Fill any empty cups about half-full with water. (That helps to keep the pan from warping in the heat of the oven.)

7. With an adult's help, put the muffin pan in the oven. Bake for 10 minutes.

8. Using potholders, take the muffin pan out of the oven. Check to see if the eggs are as cooked as you like them. If not, put the pan back in the oven for another minute and then check again.

9. To serve, run a table knife around the edge of each baked egg to loosen it from the pan. Using a fork, reach down under each egg, and then carefully lift it up out of the muffin pan and put it on a plate.

Yummy Chicken Noodle Soup

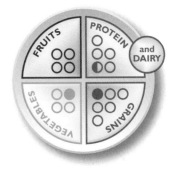

Makes 6 servings • Prep Time: 25-30 minutes
Cooking Time: 20-30 minutes

INGREDIENTS

1 medium onion

2 celery ribs

1 medium carrot

2 cups water

Two 14½-ounce cans low-fat, low-sodium chicken broth

1 teaspoon salt, *if you wish*

½ teaspoon pepper

2 cups cooked chicken

8 ounces whole-wheat noodles

Fresh parsley

EQUIPMENT

Cutting board

Knife

Large saucepan with lid

Wooden spoon

1. With an adult helping you, chop onion and celery. Slice carrot. Put vegetables in the saucepan.

2. Add water, broth, salt if you wish, and pepper. With an adult's help, turn on the heat to medium. Put the lid on the pot.

3. When the soup boils (makes big bubbles), turn the heat to low. Keep the soup cooking at a low boil (simmer) for 10-12 minutes, or until the vegetables are tender-crisp.

4. Take off the lid. With an adult helping you, take the pan off the stove. Add the chicken and noodles to the saucepan. Stir well.

5. Keep the lid off and simmer the soup until the noodles are soft, about 10-12 minutes.

6. Sprinkle with parsley and serve.

101

Tuna Flippers

Makes 8 servings • Prep Time: 40 minutes
Cooking Time: 7-9 minutes

INGREDIENTS

2 large carrots

1 tablespoon water

3 teaspoons chopped fresh parsley

Juice and zest of 1 lemon

2 egg whites, lightly beaten

½ teaspoon dried dill weed

¼ teaspoon pepper

Two 6-ounce cans water-packed tuna, drained

1½ tablespoons olive oil

EQUIPMENT

Knife

Cutting board

Microwave-safe glass bowl with lid

Potholders

Fork

Tongs

Mixing bowl

Kitchen shears

Small-hole grater or zester

Citrus juicer

2 large plates

Large skillet

Spatula

1. With an adult's help, lay each carrot on the cutting board and cut into chunks.

2. Put carrot chunks and water in the glass bowl and cover with the lid. Microwave on high for 3 minutes. Using potholders, remove the bowl.

3. Try to stick a fork in the thickest part of the carrots. If they're not soft, microwave for another minute. Try to poke the carrots again. Keep doing this until the carrots are soft.

4. Take the carrots out of the water with the tongs and place them in the mixing bowl.

5. Use the fork to mash the carrots completely.

6. Wash the parsley. Shake off the water. Use the kitchen shears to snip the parsley into little pieces. Add to the carrots.

7. Rub the whole lemon over a small-hole grater, grating off the yellow part. Or pull a zester firmly over the whole lemon to pull off the yellow part. Watch your fingers! When you're done, the lemon should be mostly white. Put the yellow zest in the glass bowl with the carrots and parsley.

8. Ask an adult to help you cut the lemon in half. Use the citrus juicer to get all the juice out. Add that to the bowl, too.

9. Ask an adult to help you crack the eggs and separate the whites from the yolks. Add egg whites, dill, pepper and tuna to the bowl. Mix it up.

10. Divide the mixture into 8 mounds. Shape each one into a round patty. Put on a large plate.

11. Ask an adult to help you heat the oil over medium heat in the skillet. Carefully put the patties in the hot skillet so they aren't touching each other. They may not all fit in at once. Just do them in batches if you need to.

12. Let them cook for 4-5 minutes until they're lightly browned on one side.

13. Ask an adult to help you use the spatula to flip the patties. Continue cooking until they're browned on the other side, about 3-4 minutes.

14. Put the finished patties on a plate. Time to eat!

Serving Suggestion: *Eat these tuna flippers like a hamburger with a whole-grain bun and fixin's, or put each one on a plate with your favorite vegetable.*

Sloppy Joes

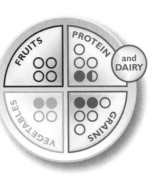

Makes 4 servings • Prep Time: 40 minutes
Cooking Time: 20 minutes

INGREDIENTS

1 cup chopped onion

1 medium bell pepper, chopped

1 medium zucchini, *if you like; not included in the nutritional analysis*

¾ pound lean ground pork loin

1½ cups canned diced tomatoes, no salt added, undrained

1 tablespoon chili powder

1 teaspoon paprika

½ teaspoon minced garlic, *if you like; not included in the nutritional analysis*

Pepper to taste

3 tablespoons tomato paste

4 whole-wheat hamburger buns

EQUIPMENT

Cutting board

Knife

Large nonstick skillet with lid

Kitchen shears

Grater

Wooden spoon

Safety can opener

Timer

1. Ask an adult to help you chop the onion. Put in the skillet.

2. Snip the bell pepper into chunks with the kitchen shears. Add them to the skillet.

3. If you want to include the zucchini, ask an adult to help you shred it with the grater. Watch your fingers! Set the grated zucchini aside.

4. Put the pork in the skillet. With an adult helping you, cook over medium heat. Stir often. Break up the clumps of pork with the wooden spoon. When the pork is no longer pink, turn off the heat.

5. Ask an adult to drain off the fat from the skillet.

6. Add tomatoes, chili powder, paprika, garlic if you wish, and pepper. Stir. Add zucchini now if you wish. Put the skillet back on the stove. Turn the heat to medium again.

7. Put the lid on the skillet. Check every few minutes to see if it's boiling (bubbling).

8. When the mixture begins to bubble, stir in the tomato paste with an adult helping you. Turn the heat down to low — the Sloppy Joes will simmer now, instead of boil. Keep the lid off. Set the timer for 5 minutes. Let the Sloppy Joes simmer until the timer buzzes.

9. Turn off the heat. Remove the pan from the stove. Stir the sauce. Spoon the meat mixture onto the buns. Serve, along with lots of napkins.

Crispy Chicken Fingers

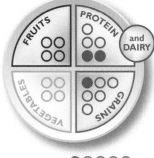

Makes 6 servings • Prep Time: 40 minutes
Cooking Time: 20 minutes

FATS ●○○○○
SWEETS ◑

INGREDIENTS

1 cup Italian bread crumbs

2 tablespoons grated Parmesan cheese

2 tablespoons vegetable oil

1 garlic clove, minced, *if you wish; not included in nutritional analysis*

6 boneless skinless chicken breast halves (about 2 pounds)

Honey-mustard sauce:

2 tablespoons cornstarch

1 cup water, *divided*

½ cup honey *or* agave nectar

¼ cup yellow mustard

EQUIPMENT

Baking sheet

Cooking spray

Quart-size plastic bag

Small bowl

Cutting board

Plastic wrap

Rolling pin

Kitchen shears

Saucepan

Whisk

Babies shouldn't eat honey. Use agave nectar instead.

1. Preheat the oven to 350° F. Spray the baking sheet with cooking spray.

2. In a plastic bag, mix the bread crumbs and cheese with your fingers. Set the bag aside.

3. Put the oil in a small bowl. Mix in the garlic if you're using it. Set the bowl aside.

4. Put the chicken on a cutting board. Cover it with plastic wrap. Flatten the chicken to ½-inch thickness by whacking it with a rolling pin.

5. Using the kitchen shears, cut each flattened chicken piece into ¼-inch wide strips. Wash your hands. Set aside everything that touched the raw chicken to be washed.

6. Dip a chicken strip in the oil in the bowl.

7. Put the coated strip into the bag of crumb mixture. Close the bag. Now squeeze the bag gently around the strip to coat it well.

8. Place the coated strip on the baking sheet.

9. Repeat the process for each strip. Put them all on the baking sheet without letting the strips touch each other. Wash your hands.

10. With an adult helping you, put the baking sheet in the oven. Bake for 20 minutes, or until the chicken strips are golden brown.

11. While the chicken fingers are baking, make the sauce. With an adult helping you, put the cornstarch in a saucepan.

12. Add 1 tablespoon water. Using a whisk, stir until the cornstarch is dissolved. Add the honey, the mustard and the rest of the water. Stir again.

13. With an adult's help, cook on medium heat. Using a whisk, stir constantly.

14. When the sauce starts boiling (bubbling), turn off the heat.

15. Serve as a dipping sauce with the chicken fingers.

Sizzlin' Chicken Fajitas

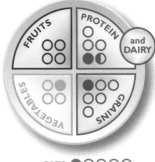

Makes 12 servings • Prep Time: 30-40 minutes
Marinating Time: 15 minutes • Cooking Time: 6-8 minutes

FATS ●○○○○

INGREDIENTS

¼ cup lime juice

1 teaspoon chili powder

½ teaspoon ground cumin

1-2 garlic cloves, minced,
 *if you wish; not included
 in nutritional analysis*

3 pounds boneless skinless
 chicken breasts

Half a green bell pepper

Half a red bell pepper

1 large onion

12 whole-wheat tortillas,
 8 inches in diameter

½ cup salsa, mild *or* spicy

½ cup fat-free sour cream

½ cup of your favorite
 low-fat shredded cheese

EQUIPMENT

Medium bowl

Kitchen shears

Wooden spoon

Cutting board

Knife

Large nonstick skillet

1. Mix lime juice, chili powder
and cumin in a medium bowl. Add garlic if you wish.

2. Using the kitchen shears, cut the chicken into ¼-inch
strips. Put the chicken strips in the juice mixture and stir
until all the chicken strips are coated. Set aside for 15
minutes to let the chicken marinate (absorb the flavor).

3. Meanwhile, ask an adult to help you core the peppers.
Using the kitchen shears, snip the peppers into thin slivers.

4. With an adult's help, slice the onion.

5. With an adult's help, heat a large nonstick skillet over
medium high heat. Spoon in the chicken and sauce (marinade).
Cook and stir for 3 minutes, or until no longer pink.

6. Add onion and peppers. Cook 3-5 minutes, stirring
occasionally, until the peppers and onion are tender-crisp.
Cook them longer if you want them softer. Turn off the heat.

7. Warm the tortillas in the microwave on high for 15-30
seconds.

8. Carefully divide the chicken mixture evenly among the
tortillas.

9. Top each tortilla with 2 teaspoons each of salsa, sour
cream and shredded cheese. Roll up and serve.

Chocolate Pudding
Page 118

Pizza Popcorn
Page 116

Sweet and Fruity
Chips 'n' Salsa
Page 114

Wacky Chocolate Cake
Page 122

Raspberry Chocolate Scones
Page 120

Chapter 5

Tiny Treats
for Now and Then

After-School Apples and Peanut Butter

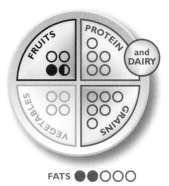

FATS ●●○○○

Makes 4 servings • Prep Time: 35 minutes

INGREDIENTS

1 green or yellow apple

1 red apple

1 small banana

½ cup grapes, cut in half

¼ cup smooth natural peanut butter

2 tablespoons skim milk

2 teaspoons brown sugar

½ teaspoon lemon juice

2 tablespoons crushed unsalted peanuts

EQUIPMENT

Cutting board

Knife

Serving bowl

Small bowl

Wooden spoon

Small whisk

Plastic sandwich bag

Rolling pin, or a can

1. Ask an adult to help you cut the grapes in half and chop up the apples. (Don't peel the apples, or you'll lose their beautiful color.) Put them in the serving bowl.

2. Peel the banana. Ask an adult to help you slice the banana. Put in the serving bowl.

3. Make the dressing. Put peanut butter, milk, sugar and lemon juice in the small bowl. Whisk gently until everything is smooth.

4. Pour the dressing over the fruit in the serving bowl. Mix gently.

5. Put peanuts into a plastic sandwich bag and close it up. Crush peanuts by rolling a rolling pin or a can back and forth over the nuts.

6. Sprinkle smashed peanuts over the fruit and serve.

Alert!
Don't make this recipe for someone who has a peanut allergy.

Sweet and Fruity Chips 'n' Salsa

SWEETS ◑

Makes 10 servings (a serving is 8 pieces) • Prep Time: 35 minutes
Cooking Time: 10-12 minutes • Chilling Time: 2-3 hours

INGREDIENTS

Tortilla crisps:

8 whole-wheat tortillas

1 tablespoon sugar

½ tablespoon cinnamon

Fruit salsa:

3 cups diced fresh fruit — apples, oranges, kiwi, strawberries, grapes *or* other fresh fruit that you like

2 tablespoons sugar-free jam that you like

1 tablespoon honey *or* agave nectar

2 tablespoons orange juice

EQUIPMENT

Kitchen shears

Cooking spray

2 baking sheets

2 small bowls

Spoon

Potholders

Cooling rack

Knife

Cutting board

Medium mixing bowl

Small whisk

Wooden spoon

Plastic wrap

Babies shouldn't eat honey. Use agave nectar instead.

1. Preheat the oven to 350° F.

2. Cut each tortilla into 10 wedges with the kitchen shears. Spread over baking sheets without piling them up. Spray the pieces with cooking spray, being sure to hit each one.

3. In one of the small bowls, combine sugar and cinnamon. Sprinkle evenly over the tortilla wedges.

4. With an adult's help, put the baking sheets in the oven. Bake 10-12 minutes, or until the pieces are crisp.

5. With an adult helping you, and using potholders, take the baking sheets out of the oven. Place on a cooling rack and let the chips cool.

6. With an adult's help, cut the fruit into cubes. Gently mix the cut-up fruit together in the mixing bowl.

7. In a separate small bowl, mix jam, honey and orange juice using the small whisk.

8. Pour this sauce over the diced fruit. Mix gently.

9. Cover the bowl with plastic wrap. Refrigerate for 2-3 hours.

10. Serve as a dip or topping for the cinnamon tortilla chips.

Pizza Popcorn

Makes about 12 cups (a serving is 2 cups) • Prep Time: 25 minutes

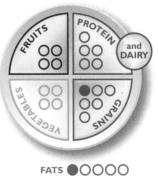

FATS ●○○○○

INGREDIENTS

3 quarts air-popped popcorn

3 tablespoons canola oil

2 tablespoons grated reduced-fat Parmesan cheese

1 teaspoon garlic powder

1 teaspoon Italian herb seasoning

1 teaspoon paprika

Dash of pepper, *if you like*

EQUIPMENT

Large mixing bowl

Wooden spoon

1. Put popcorn in the large bowl. Pour oil over it. Mix the oil and the popcorn as well as you can with a wooden spoon.

2. Sprinkle with the rest of the ingredients. Then stir again, trying to get some of the toppings on each piece of popped corn.

3. Enjoy!

Chocolate Pudding

Makes 4 servings • Prep Time: 15 minutes • Chilling Time: 1-1¼ hours

FATS ◑○○○○

INGREDIENTS

3½ cups cold skim milk

Two 2.1-ounce packages sugar-free chocolate pudding

½ cup fat-free sour cream

1 teaspoon almond extract

4 tablespoons chopped nuts, *if you like; not included in nutritional analysis*

EQUIPMENT

Metal mixing bowl

Whisk

Serving spoon

4 dessert bowls

Plastic wrap

1. Put the metal mixing bowl in the freezer for 10-20 minutes.

2. When the bowl is chilled, pour in milk, pudding mix, sour cream and almond extract.

3. Using a whisk, stir until the mixture thickens.

4. Divide the pudding among 4 small dessert bowls. Cover each bowl with plastic wrap.

5. Set the bowls in the refrigerator for at least 1 hour. Sprinkle with nuts, if you like, before serving.

Raspberry Chocolate Scones

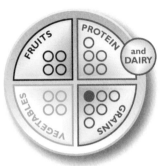

Makes 12 servings • Prep Time: 15 minutes • Cooking Time: 10-12 minutes

FATS ●○○○○
SWEETS ◐

INGREDIENTS

1 cup whole-wheat pastry flour

1 cup all-purpose flour

1 tablespoon baking powder

¼ teaspoon baking soda

⅓ cup trans-fat-free margarine

½ cup fresh *or* frozen raspberries

¼ cup miniature chocolate chips

1 cup plus 2 tablespoons plain fat-free yogurt

2 tablespoons honey *or* agave nectar

½ teaspoon sugar

¼ teaspoon cinnamon

EQUIPMENT

Baking sheet

Cooking spray

Large mixing bowl

Wooden spoon

Pastry cutter

2 small bowls

Rolling pin

Ruler

Table knife

Potholders

Cooling rack

1. Preheat the oven to 400° F. Spray the baking sheet lightly with cooking spray.

2. Mix both flours, baking powder and baking soda in a large mixing bowl.

3. Using the pastry cutter, cut in the margarine until the mixture turns into pieces about the size of peas.

4. Add berries and chocolate chips. Mix very gently.

5. Mix yogurt and honey together in a small bowl.

6. Add the yogurt mixture to the flour mixture, mixing until they're mostly blended. It will be hard to stir.

7. Spill the dough out onto the countertop. Fold the dough in half and push it down hard with the heels of your hands. Turn the dough and repeat the folding and pushing. Do this 1 or 2 more times. You have just kneaded the dough!

8. The dough should now be one solid ball. Using the rolling pin, roll it into a circle that is ½-inch thick. Use a ruler to check — the baking time is based on this thickness.

9. With the table knife, cut the circle into 12 wedges as you would cut a pizza.

10. Place the wedges on the baking sheet, spaced as far apart from each other as possible.

11. Mix sugar and cinnamon together in another small bowl. Sprinkle the mixture over the wedges.

12. With an adult helping you, put the baking sheet in the oven. Bake for 10-12 minutes.

13. With an adult's help, and using potholders, take the baking sheet out of the oven and put on the cooling rack.

14. Serve cooled to room temperature or chilled.

Babies shouldn't eat honey. Use agave nectar instead.

Wacky Chocolate Cake

Makes 20 servings • Prep Time: 20 minutes • Cooking Time: 30 minutes

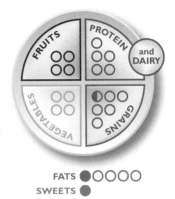

FATS ●○○○○
SWEETS ●

INGREDIENTS

3 cups whole-wheat pastry flour

1 cup sugar

3 tablespoons unsweetened cocoa powder

½ teaspoon salt

2¼ teaspoons baking soda

1 tablespoon vanilla

2 tablespoons vinegar

½ cup canola oil

2 cups water

EQUIPMENT

9-by-13-inch baking pan

Whisk

Wooden spoon

2-cup glass measuring cup

Potholders

Cooling rack

Table knife

This cake is delicious topped with sliced bananas, vanilla yogurt, applesauce or a sprinkling of powdered sugar.

1. Preheat the oven to 350° F.

2. Put flour, sugar, cocoa powder, salt and baking soda directly into the ungreased baking pan.

3. Use the whisk to stir them all together.

4. Using the wooden spoon, make 3 separate holes in the dry ingredients.

5. Pour the vanilla into one hole. Pour the vinegar into another hole. Pour the oil into the third hole. (Isn't this wacky?)

6. Put the water in a 2-cup glass measuring cup. Microwave on high for 3 minutes, or until the water is bubbling.

7. Ask an adult to carefully take the cup out of the microwave and to pour the boiling water slowly and evenly over the ingredients in the pan.

8. Use the whisk to mix everything together for 2 minutes. It should be completely mixed, with no traces of dry ingredients.

9. With an adult helping you, put the baking pan in the oven. Bake for 25-30 minutes, or until a toothpick stuck into the center of the cake comes out clean.

10. With an adult's help, and using potholders, take the pan out of the oven and put it on a cooling rack.

11. When the cake is completely cooled, cut into 20 squares with a table knife. Time to serve!

Glossary

Beat – Stir fast with a spoon, fork, whisk or electric mixer in order to make a mixture smooth.

Boil – Cook a liquid to such a hot temperature that big bubbles appear.

Broken yolks – The result of whisking an egg yolk so that it is no longer whole. The yellow center becomes runny.

Chop – Cut food into small pieces.

Coat – Completely cover the surface of a food with another food.

Cover – Put a lid or sheet of foil, waxed paper or plastic wrap over food.

Crack eggs – Tap the egg on the side of a bowl. Then, working over a bowl, pull the eggshell halves apart and let the egg white and yolk fall into the bowl. (Do not let the shell fall into the bowl!)

Dice – Chop food into small, square, even-sized pieces.

Divide – Separate individual ingredients into smaller batches.

Drain – Pour off a liquid in which a food has been cooked or stored.

Grease – Rub the inside of baking dishes and pans with butter or oil, or spray them with cooking spray, so that food baked in them won't stick.

Layer – Stack one food item on top of another.

Melt – Heat something solid until it becomes a liquid.

Mince – Cut food into very small pieces.

Mix – Stir ingredients with a spoon, fork, whisk or mixer until smooth or well blended.

Prick – Lightly poke food with a fork so hot air can escape from inside the food.

Scrape – Use a spatula to clean food out of a bowl or container.

Set – When a liquid becomes more solid as it cooks or cools.

Sprinkle – Scatter an ingredient lightly over top of something.

Stir – Mix with a spoon.

Tender-Crisp – Food that is cooked until it's slightly softened, yet still somewhat crunchy.

Thaw – When a frozen food item warms up enough so that it's no longer frozen.

Undrained – When the liquid in which a food is cooked or stored is kept, rather than being poured away.

Whisk – Mix in a circular motion using a whisk.

Index

Index

About Mayo Clinic

Mayo Clinic is the first and largest integrated, not-for-profit group practice in the world, and provides health and wellness services to consumers and businesses across the globe. Joined by common systems and a philosophy that "the needs of the patient come first," more than 3,700 doctors and scientists from every medical specialty, and over 50,000 allied health staff work together to care for patients, conduct medical research, and train tomorrow's health care providers. Each year, Mayo Clinic treats more than half a million people from all walks of life at its campuses in Rochester, Minn.; Jacksonville, Fla.; and Phoenix/Scottsdale, Ariz., and via community-based providers in more than 70 locations in the Upper Midwest.

My Cookbook Diary

I made this recipe	Date when I made the recipe	How the recipe turned out

My Cookbook Diary

I made this recipe	Date when I made the recipe	How the recipe turned out
....	....	....
....	....	....
....	....	....
....	....	....
....	....	....
....	....	....
....	....	....
....	....	....
....	....	....
....	....	....
....	....	....
....	....	....
....	....	....
....	....	....
....	....	....
....	....	....
....	....	....
....	....	....